# Nine Hymns for the Church Year

## Arranged for Organ
## by James Pethel

Editor: Dale Tucker
Art Design: Thais Yanes

# Contents

# COME, THOU LONG-EXPECTED JESUS

**Hyfrydol**

SW: Solo Reed 8'
GT: Principals 8', 4', 2', Mixture
PED: Bourdons 16', 8', Gt. to Ped.

Hymn Tune by
ROWLAND H. PRICHARD
*Arranged by*
JAMES PETHEL (ASCAP)

**With movement, but not fast**

GBM0310

slight rit.
Sw.
a tempo
ff
Gt.
GBM0310

6
Sw.
simile
Gt.
GBM0310

(hold back)
ff
Slower
rit.
molto rit.

# AH, HOLY JESUS

**Choral: Herzliebster Jesu**

SW:  String 8', Flute 8'
PED: Solo Reed 4', (trem.)

Hymn Tune by
JOHANN HEERMAN
*Arranged by*
*JAMES PETHEL (ASCAP)*

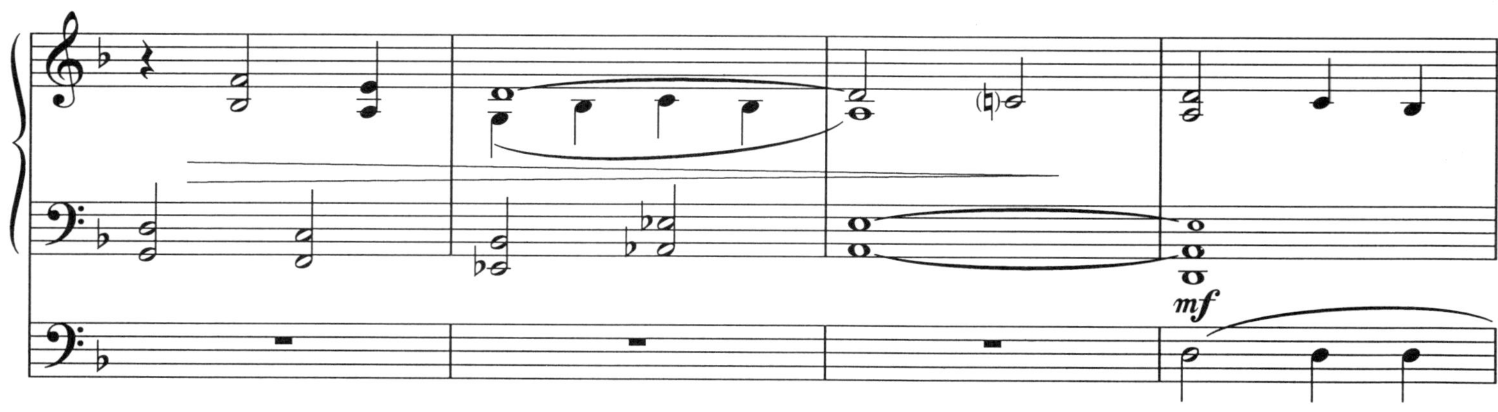

GBM0310

*The F may be played with or without the sharp at the discretion of the organist.

# Toccata on
# COME, THOU FOUNT OF EVERY BLESSING

**Warrenton**

SW:  Full
GT:  Full, Sw. to Gt.
PED: Bourdon 16', Sw. to Ped.

Tune from
Wyeth's Repository of Sacred Music, Part II
*Arranged by*
*JAMES PETHEL (ASCAP)*

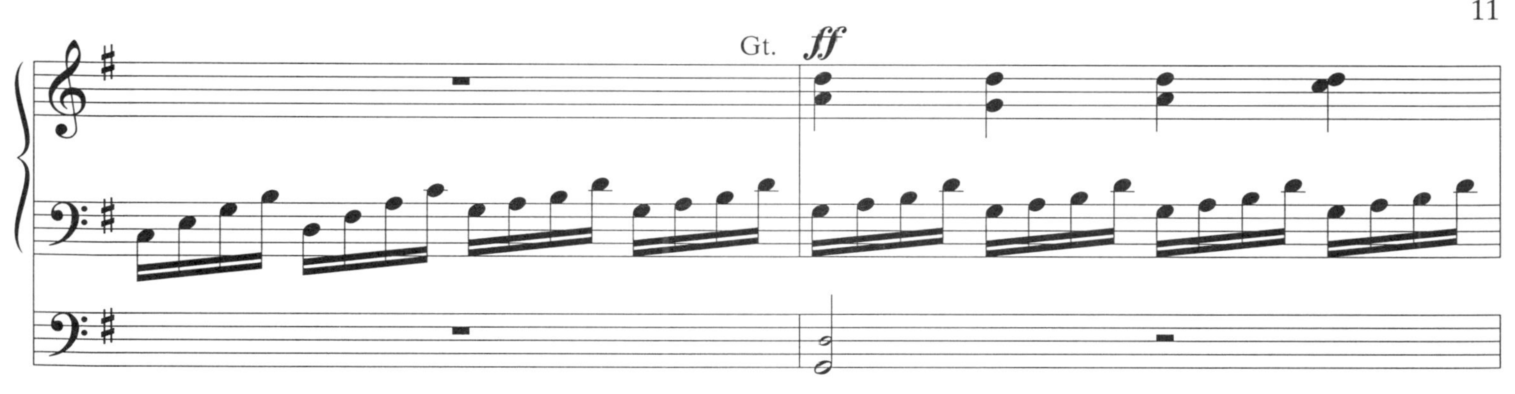
Gt.
ff

Sw.
Sw.

Gt.

Sw. mf

Gt.
Sw.

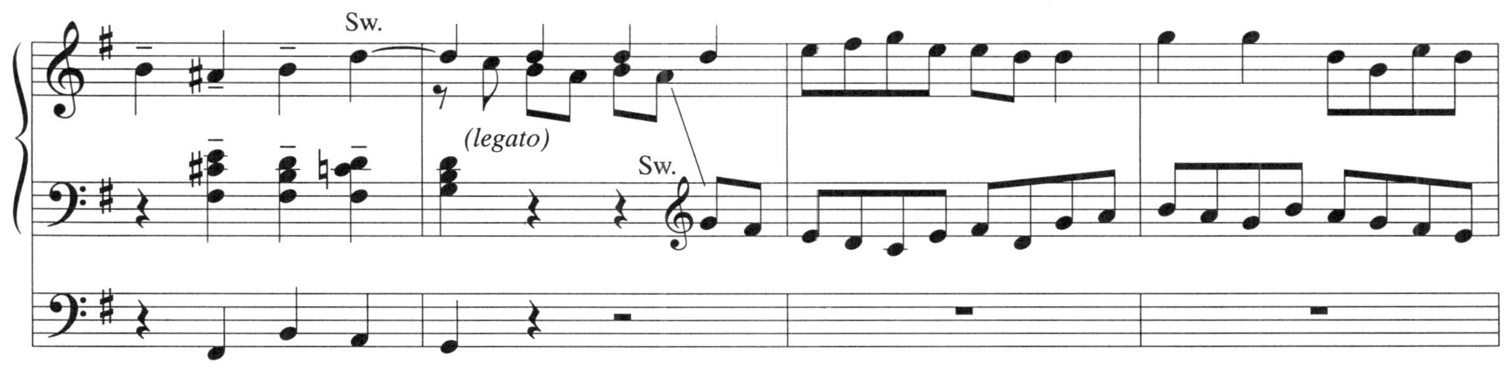

GBM0310

ten.
rit.
a tempo
cresc. e accel.

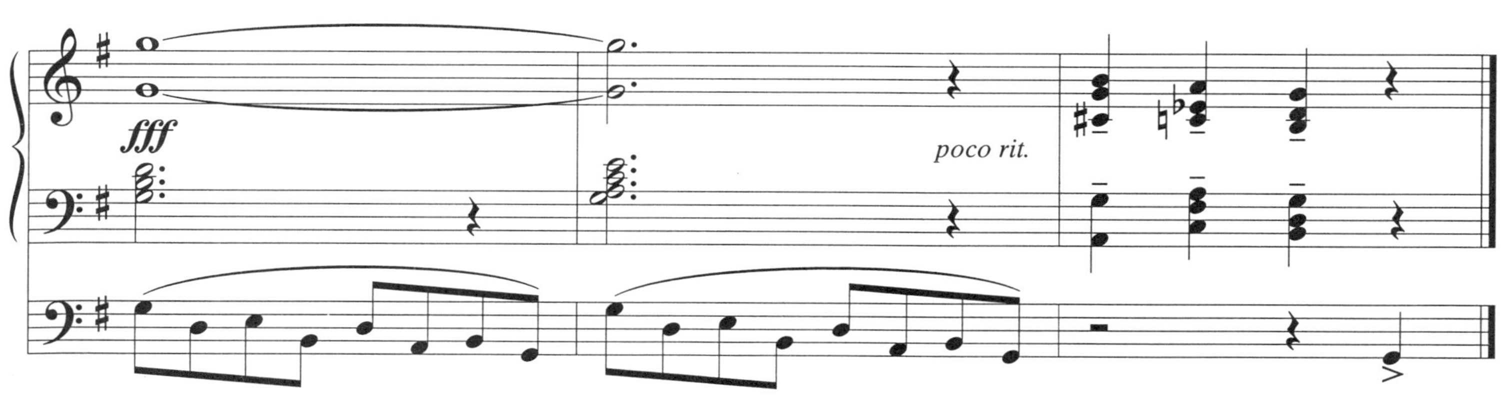
fff
poco rit.

# DING! DONG! MERRILY WE SING

## French Carol

GBM0310

add Prins. 8', 4'
Sw.
f
legato

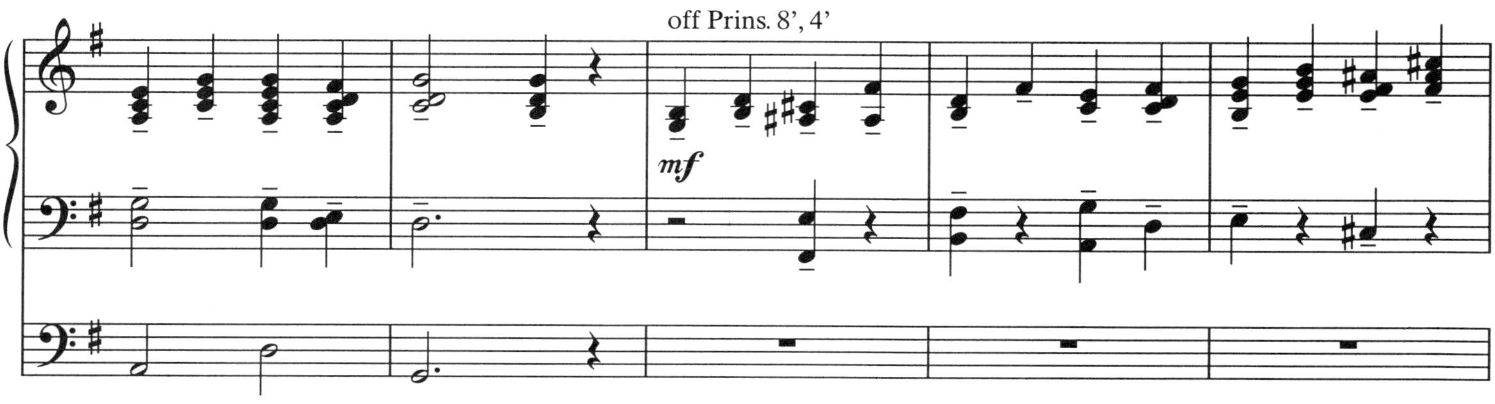
off Prins. 8', 4'
mf

Gt.
simile
add Prins. 8', 4'
Sw. f
rit.

*Optional: Handbell choir may double manuals ad lib. as desired.

ten.
poco rit.
Tempo I
add Prins. 4', 2'
Gt.
f
rit.
add Gt. to Ped.
Presto
a tempo
tutti
add Reeds 16', 8'

# JERUSALEM, THE GOLDEN

**Ewing**



Hymn Tune by
ALEXANDER EWING
*Arranged by*
*JAMES PETHEL (ASCAP)*

GBM0310

Gt.
f
Sw.
rit.
mp
(freely)
p
Gt.
mp
rit.
a tempo
molto rit.
pp

# MORE LOVE TO THEE

SW: Flutes 8', 4'
GT: Solo stop 8'
PED: 16', 8'

Hymn Tune by
**WILLIAM H. DOANE**
*Arranged by*
*JAMES PETHEL (ASCAP)*

**Slowly, but flowing**

Sw.
Gt.

# THIS IS MY FATHER'S WORLD
## Terra Beata

25
f add Prins. 8', 4'
Sw.
f
off Prins. 8', 4'
GBM0310

add Prins. 8', 4'
f
Flutes 8', 4'
Sw.
mp
Gt.
mf
off Prins.
Adagio
Sw. String & Celeste 8'
rit.
p

Commissioned by the First United Methodist Church of Maryville, TN
Honoring Dwain Pesterfield for his 25 years of service as organist.

# TO GOD BE THE GLORY

SW: Full with Reeds
GT: Principals 8', 4', Mixture, Reeds
PED: Principals 16', 8', Gt. to Ped.

Hymn Tune by
WILLIAM H. DOANE
*Arranged by*
*JAMES PETHEL (ASCAP)*

Sw.
mp
Gt.
Sw.
mp
Gt.
add Sw. to Gt.
ff

Sw.: Fls. 8', 4'
mf
(detached)
mp
Gt. Prin. 8'
f
3

Gt. (legato)
rit.

Broadly
add Prins. 4', 2', Mixt.
f
add Bright Reeds
a tempo
Sw.
f
add Reeds 16', 8'
ff
Gt.
Sw.
Gt.

Full Organ
ff
rit.

# Introduction, Fughetta, and Hymn on
# RISE UP O CHURCH OF GOD!

**St. Thomas**

SW: Full with Reeds
GT: Principals 8', 4', Mixture, Reeds, Sw. to Gt.
PED: 16', 8', Gt. to Ped.

Hymn Tune by
AARON WILLIAMS
*Arranged by*
*JAMES PETHEL (ASCAP)*

GBM0310

Sw. (box closed)
rit.
a tempo
mf
3

f

Gt.
add Reeds 16', 8'
ff

Maestoso
rit.
ff
ten.
ten.